Nan the Red ~

By Jebb McFlickers

Illustrated by Philomena O'Neil

Target Skill Short Ee/e/

PEARSON

Scott
Foresman

Nan is a red hen.

She is in a red pen.

Nan spots Ken.

He is not in a pen.

Can Nan get to Ken?

Go, Nan, go!

Here, Nan, here!

Nan can go from here to Ken.

Nan can get to Ken.